Divalution

Divalution

The Evolution and Revolution of the Diva

Deborah St.Hilaire

authorHOUSE®

AuthorHouse™
1663 Liberty Drive
Bloomington, IN 47403
www.authorhouse.com
Phone: 1-800-839-8640

Published by AuthorHouse   10/26/2012

ISBN: 978-1-4772-8478-0 (sc)
ISBN: 978-1-4772-8480-3 (hc)
ISBN: 978-1-4772-8479-7 (e)

Library of Congress Control Number: 2012920217

Any people depicted in stock imagery provided by Thinkstock are models, and such images are being used for illustrative purposes only.
Certain stock imagery © Thinkstock.

This book is printed on acid-free paper.

Because of the dynamic nature of the Internet, any web addresses or links contained in this book may have changed since publication and may no longer be valid. The views expressed in this work are solely those of the author and do not necessarily reflect the views of the publisher, and the publisher hereby disclaims any responsibility for them.

This is an excerpt from "Divaisms" by me and Christine Chapman. I am including it because I have to tell you more.

Diva to Diva

You know how sometimes a chance meeting with someone changes your life? You cross paths with a woman you admire and make her your mentor, often times without her even knowing it. I was fortunate enough to meet such a woman when I was nine months old. She not only became my mentor, she became my mother. I thank God every day for bringing my parents to me. However, I don't think I have ever thanked them. It is too late to tell my dad, but he always knew. My mom and I didn't get along very well. I have never really told her how grateful I am. This is to her, before it is too late.

Dear Mom,

It wasn't until I became the mother of a teenager that I truly understood the dynamics of our relationship. I am sorry for being so strong willed. You handled it well and taught me that I couldn't always have my way. There are many words left unsaid between us. After you read this there will not be any. I am sorry that I waited this long to say them.

I doubt that you know how grateful I am for you and dad. Thank you for choosing me to be your daughter and never making me feel adopted. Thank you for your honesty. Thank you for your time. My childhood was wonderful. I remember all the little things you did for us, all the places we went. I don't know how you did it and still ran a successful business. My life was full of fun and laughter. Most of all I thank you of the unconditional love you have given me. You have always been there for me. Throughout my entire life you have supported me, allowing me to fail without questioning my decisions and loving me in spite of them.

You have been my source of strength, my one constant, and my only refuge. During the hard times of my life, and there have been quite a few, I would picture myself on your lap in a rocking chair and make it through somehow. You have given me my faith, my sense of humor, my trust in others and the ability to be a good mother.

You were the first true Diva I ever knew. You gave my sister and me the greatest gift we will ever receive: The opportunity to follow in your path with you holding our hands. Thank you, not for giving me life, but for giving me your life.

I love you mom,

Your Eldest Daughter

Deborah St.Hilaire

Now, I would like to tell you about my mother, Helen Veronica Pachipka Makidon. She was a Pennsylvania farm girl with 12 siblings, a coal miner/farmer father and a humble, stern yet loving mother. She was Czechoslovakian, the first generation to be born in America. She had full lips and high cheek bones, wore red lip stick, had freckles and dyed her hair red. Yep, she was a Diva.

What a family!! I had Aunts and Uncles who were more like parents and cousins who were closer than most brothers and sisters. We had dinner together several times a week, went on group vacations and spent the summer in a tent and camper with different sets of parents tending to us. I later found out that the other sets of parents would go on day trips or romantic get-aways.

We had a lower middle class home, high roller vacations and private Catholic schools. She and my father worked as janitors to afford the tuition. They invested in us, made our memories and created a strong sense of who we were without ever saying a word.

She and my Aunt Margie owned a catering company. Those women could cook! We all helped. Most of the time it was fun. I used to watch my mom interact with all sorts of people in countless situations. She seldom lost her temper but when she did . . . all hell broke loose. She laughed a lot with her siblings, my daddy and us. She would throw her head back and her tongue would creep between her teeth. She was nice to everyone. When she told a joke, she could never remember the punch line. She often wore a flower in her hair when she was young. She had a wooden sign in the kitchen that said "Housework makes you ugly" and a white dish with gold lettering that read "It's my house and I'll do as I damn well please". She talked to everyone and gave away food to as many people as possible. She was generous beyond her means and selfless when it came to her family. She was quite a woman.

I can remember when she learned to drive and swim. She was a character, always ready to learn something new. I got spanked a lot growing up, slapped for talking back and grounded for not listening, but it wasn't until I became a teen ager that we butted heads horribly. She used to say that she couldn't tell me what to do from the time I was three years old. I believe it.

Anyway, one summer week end, when I was in my forties, Christine and I rented a big old house and had a Diva retreat. I invited my sister and cousins and mom offered to take care of my boys. We had ten or so women there. On Sunday morning, the last morning of the retreat, I invited mom over for brunch with us. All of the women there were connected with her. I read the above excerpt to her. We both cried, everyone did. We were so much closer after that.

Ten years later we got the news that her health was quickly deteriorating. Her last four months were spent in a wheel chair. Diabetes had finally taken its toll on that worn out body. She had the option of having her leg amputated but whispered to me that she wanted to see daddy "whole", that if it wasn't that leg, it would soon be something else that would be the end of her. How could I argue with that? We knew she was in pain but she seldom complained. She lived with my remarkable sister and bighearted brother-in-law. I was there three days a week. We talked, laughed till tears came, ate good food, played cards and beauty shop while we watched her slipping from us. She was right. The other leg got infected.

When she passed, I looked at my sister and said "Well we've come full circle, we're orphans again", she replied "but now we have each other".

It has been nearly four years ago. That beautiful woman lived with full out gusto. She left us with a head full of memories and a heart full of love. She was the first Diva I ever met. She was true to herself. She loved unconditionally. How lucky I am to have known her. I miss her every day.

This book is for and because of the wonderful women who raised me. My grandmother, mother, sister, aunts and cousins, who taught me how to give freely, love unconditionally, laugh uncontrollably, be myself and fight for what I believe in. Thank you.

To My Mothers

Deborah St. Hilaire was adopted when she was nine months old and began a journey that took her to Canada, California, Europe, back to her home state of Ohio, then to Michigan, where she currently resides with her husband. She has worn many hats, from dog groomer to aerobics instructor to Realtor and all things in between. She has traveled extensively. Wherever she went, she met, observed and recorded. She has been divorced three times, bounced back from financial devastation, healed many broken hearts and has learned along the way. Deborah is a Diva, life and design psychology coach, motivational speaker, owner of "skys the limit", co-owner of "Women Empowered", poet, artist and author. Her greatest accomplishments are her two sons.

Deborah also co authored a book with Christine Chapman called "Divaisms".

She is currently developing a high school program, for young women and men titled "The Divalutionary Evolutionary Wars: the training of the troops" in hopes that the next generation can get it right.

It's in the reach of my arms

The span of my hips,

The stride of my step,

The curl of my lips.

I'm a woman

Phenomenally.

Phenomenal woman,

That's me.

MAYA ANGELOU, *Phenomenal Woman*

Background

About ten years ago my dear friend, Christine, and I set out on a mission to raise the collective spirit of womanhood. We saw what was happening in our own lives and knew we were not alone. We were losing ourselves in our children, our partners, our work and our homes. We were trying to do it all and leaving very little time for our own interests and self nurturing and no time at all for pampering.

To make matters worse, we women were working against each other in the work place and on the home front. There was back biting, vicious gossip and affairs with married men. There was depression, a higher risk of disease, panic attacks, self loathing, destruction and stress. I witnessed women disgracing their friends instead of supporting them, shunning women who had mentored them and successful women becoming thankless and rude. We were becoming cannibalistic.

What had happened, to us, in a mere generation? True, we had become stronger but at what cost? We were becoming men, me included.

This is what our book, "Divisims" addressed. We wanted to raise the universal awareness of this peril we had brought upon ourselves and change it! We wanted women to choose the high road.

We failed. Perhaps we, collectively, had not evolved enough to alter the path. Perhaps we were ahead of our time. My only hope that now is not too late. Maybe more of us are ready to take a long hard look.

Christine has graciously allowed me to try again, with many of the same words. I am grateful that she still has faith in our original intent and in me. Thank you, Christine.

So, here I go again. With ten more years under my expensive leather belt, a few more wrinkles, much more gray hair and so many more divastations.

Join me, ladies.

Let the Divalution begin!

Gratitude

I owe so much to so many.

There have been times in my life when my mere survival depended on the others.

My sister, Regina, and her husband George. My "brother", Mike, and his wife Mary Kay for their unwavering support in everything I have ever done. Betsy and Tim for always making me laugh and feel extraordinary. Don, for liver Sundays, a shoulder to cry on and continuous friendship. My sons, Errol and Mike, who have always inspired me to be my best and allowed me many personal Divalutions. My parents, who gave me inner strength and taught me that nothing was impossible. They not only saved me from being an orphan but gave me the most loving, wonderful family anyone could ever hope for. A family that I am both grateful for and to.

I thank every man who has ever loved me and I have ever loved. Beginning that list would be my dad, Grandpas and Uncle Andy, my cousins, my sons, ending that list is Steve, my step son and my beautiful grandsons. I could name others but that's another story.

I especially thank my Port Clinton, Ohio friends, Gina and George, Steve and Susan for knowing me well and loving me when my world was falling apart. They gave me hope. It ended up being just another Divalutionary step now happily shared from the brighter side.

It amazes me how my friends saved me without my asking. This is the world I want I for everyone. I hope that the Divalution will open your hearts to look around. If anyone needs help, please reach out to them, expecting nothing in return.

It is what Divas do!

Deborah St.Hilaire

"Woman" is my slave name; feminism will give me freedom to seek some other identity altogether.

ANN SNITOW, "A Gender Diary," *Conflicts in Feminism*

Divalution

The Evolution and Revolution of the Diva

Deborah St.Hilaire

Diva Q and A

Is one born a Diva?

A few lucky ones are. Some are raised to become Divas. More are self made. Most evolve.

All are self-proclaimed.

How does one know when she has achieved Divahood?

Oh, you'll know!

Will I know when look in the mirror?

Only if you focus on your eyes, for there lies the reflection of your Diva soul.

At what age does one become a Diva?

There is no time line . . . only a time limit.

What do Divas do?

Anything we desire . . . well and with gusto!

Does one's physical beauty dictate her Diva eligibility?

A true Diva's strength and beauty comes from within. She does, however, always make the most of her shell.

Must a Diva have money?

Yes, but the amount does not matter. A Diva is very well groomed and has her own unique sense of style. You can find it at Nordstrom's or Good Will.

Does a woman have to be a bitch to experience a Divalution?

Absolutely not! Quite the opposite is true. The Divalution is all about women coming together. It is a personal experience and a group endeavor. You must experience the evolution before you can join the revolution. Bitchiness must be put aside, unless in extreme circumstance or under personal duress. Start with the woman in the mirror. Look at her. She may appear the bitch at first glance but once you see her eyes and hear her laugh, you'll know she's part of the Divalution.

Can anyone join the Divalution?

Yes, given the right circumstances. To become a Diva, one must be unique, handle adversity well, make decisions, bounce back quickly, cherish her friends, look her best, be open to new experiences, communicate well, be willing to mentor, not gossip and live with gusto. Most importantly, to join the Divalution, a woman must see herself as she truly is and love herself not in spite of but because of.

What change will the Divalution bring about?

The personal side will allow you to become the happiest and best you can possibly be, from the inside out. The movement will put an end to the pettiness, shallowness and emptiness we have shared for far too long. That is what the Divalution is all about. It is a movement to restore you and reunite us all, as the sisters we are meant to be. So invite your mothers, daughters, sisters, aunts, cousins and friends to join you. There is great strength in numbers. It is time we became strong. It is time we became one.

My Thoughts

Deborah St.Hilaire

Decisions

If there is one thing we excel in it is making decisions. In fact, we almost do it too well. We amaze people with the rapidity of our weighing the pros and cons coming up with a rational, often brilliant conclusion. We do this removed, looking at all sides without prejudice or opinion four times faster than the average human being. We take this gift for granted because we have always had it. That is why your friends come to you with their problems. We unmuddy the waters of their minds. Where did it come from, this gift of sorting things out? Practice.

We can attribute it to parents that allowed us to make our own decisions early on even if they were not the right ones. We often learned our lessons the hard way but seldom made the same mistake twice.

Our most difficult task is not making decisions for others. We watch people think and rethink even the simplest of tasks and just want to jump right on in there and make a choice for them. We know what they should do long before they do. This is when we have to stand back, take a couple of deep breaths and help them weigh their options. The pros and cons list is a good tool for the weak of heart or the devastatingly indecisive. Teach them how to make better, quicker decisions by using that brain of theirs! This is especially true of our children.

Let's talk about our children a little here. Our job is not to mold them into the adult we want them to be but to allow them to grow into the best person they can be with strong morals, a healthy sense of self esteem and responsibility, with loyal friends, kind and capable of making a decision. Their decisions may not always be the ones we would make nor the right one for them. That's how they will learn and make a better choice next time. Each time they make a decision it will be a quicker wiser one. I suggest starting them off young.

My Thoughts

CHILDREN

How fortunate they are to have you for a mother!

Trust me, they will not always appreciate this fact, especially the daughters, during their teen years. This will shift in early adulthood. It will take distance to make them realize that you were, are and always will be their rock.

Your daughter will inherit a strong sense of herself through your example. The world will be a little easier for her to navigate and conquer. After the teenager is finished butting heads with you, the woman will request your advice and opinion. She will not always heed your advice but she will always value your opinion. She will be confident and poised. She will make you proud.

Sons will be easier. They will do the head butting with their fathers. You will be the approachable go-between. The peacemaker is a fun roll to have. They will be more open with you which gives you the opportunity to teach them good communication skills. Your challenge is to turn them into strong, competent, unencumbered men. They will grow to admire and find comfort in your feminine strength. They will not fear women with similar qualities. They will attract a good wife and have the sustenance to keep her. You will be proud of the man he will become.

From the day they are born we give our entire selves to them. We love them whole heartedly and unconditionally. There is no such thing as loving your child too much. There is, however, the inclination to give our children too much.

I have seen so many parents overindulge their children. It is understandable that we want them to have the things we never had, the life we never lived, blah blah blah blah. Our parents wanted the same for us and theirs before them. When is it going to stop?!Somewhere in there some of us forgot about giving them the things we did have, things that money cannot buy. Like unconditional love, an unsolicitated hug and kiss, our undivided attention, a sit down family dinner, at least once, during the week and always on Sundays. Our job is to give them someone to look up to with respect and admiration, a role model, a guide and teacher. Only after they are grown up on their own should we be their friend. Many of us do these things and then fall short when it comes to accountability. Chores and good grades are a part of learning how to live outside of the nest. Curfews and rules are part of becoming responsible. As adults, we are still bound by these two fundamentals of life, how can we expect an adult partner to phone home when they are late if they never learned to when they were young? It is a conscious decision to be considerate of others, one that must be taught. Everything we do and say affects the adult they will become. It's inevitable that we will make mistakes, let them be little ones.

Their financial success does not always mean that they are well adjusted. How many rich friends do you have that see a shrink on a weekly basis? There are more important attributes upon which to base your parenting skills evaluation. Here are just a few: Are they happy? Do they have good, long time friends? Do they enjoy what they do and how they live? Do they know how to love? Do they phone you just to talk? Are they affectionate toward you and other members of the family? Are they good partners and parents?

Someday, with a tear in their eye, your child will thank you. Someday, they will give back so much more than you ever expected. That is when you will be certain that your job was well done. You will be overcome with emotion.

When my first son was born I received a gift from a very dear friend. A framed watercolor of Pegasus with the following verse written over it:

"There are two things we can give our children; one is roots, the other wings."

Make sure you give them both.

Our time with them is so fleeting. Cherish every moment.

Deborah St.Hilaire

My Thoughts

Deborah St.Hilaire

How Many Divas Does It Take To Do The Work Of One Man? None!

As a Diva, this concept may sound foreign to you. Perhaps even contradictory. However, we must open our hearts and minds to this fact if we intend to invite or maintain an enduring relationship. We cannot expect ourselves to do all that a man can . . . we are women. God created us to be different for a reason and we must learn to embrace those differences. Divas must acknowledge that we want a man, not for completion, but instead companionship. We do not seek safety, we desire security. We do not require a man in order to be happy, we enjoy sharing the laughter and inside jokes. He can provide us with love and bring us to ecstasy. A fulfilling relationship is a rare and precious commodity. We know that. We value that. We are comfortable with it.

There are women who believe they are weak because they like having a man around. This is simply not true. Its fine to admit that we prefer being in a relationship. There is strength in knowing yourself. A strong monogamous relationship brings out a side of us that would lie dormant otherwise. It gives us the freedom to be ourselves. We shine just a little bit brighter and smile a bit more easily. We can be our absolute best when we have found the right partner. The key word here is "right".

Men are attracted to your strength. Don't fall for fall for fancy words and promises made too soon, for actions truly do speak louder.

The most difficult part about a new relationship is entering into it gradually. Think of it as a swim in the ocean. Dip one toe at a time. Grow accustomed to it gradually, inch by inch. Proceed cautiously, being constantly aware of the depth. Is it getting deeper? Swim around for a time; tread water watching for waves feeling for undercurrents. Don't dive in until you are certain it is safe. Hopefully, when you do go under, there will be beautiful coral formations and exotic fish. If so, stay. If not . . . get out fast! Call the lifeguard. There will be another man just waiting.

I guess what I am trying to say is proceed cautiously and with discretion. Get to know him. Meet his friends and watch how they interact. Allow the time necessary for him to reveal his capacity to provide the things you want and need, both mentally and physically. Let him define his job description. We can only rely on a mate to provide the things he values as important in a relationship. No more, no less. Do not try to change him. Do not expect of force him to go beyond his capabilities. It will not last. You will be the one who suffers. If you are comfortable with the gaps fill them with activities, hobbies, friends and family.

Don't expect. Base the anticipation on the individual, not past experience. Always, always tell how much you love and appreciate him and the things he does. Always let him do those things. Do not try to take over or pick up the slack. The slack will become too much to handle and resentment will set in. Resentment is an ugly and destructive thing. Keep it at bay by communicating. No relationship will stay perfect. With a little effort, some relationships stay.

Let us accept the fact, without embarrassment or shame; we are at our best with the love of a good man. Realize how pleasurable shared love is. Cherish every minute. The right partner will provide the devotion and energy we crave to shine brighter than we ever imagined.

The right man will allow us to be better than we are alone. Let him.

My Thoughts

_____

_____

_____

_____

_____

_____

_____

_____

_____

_____

_____

_____

_____

_____

_____

_____

_____

_____

_____

Deborah St.Hilaire

A Divalutionary Truth

Accept the past for what it was. Acknowledge the present for what it is. Anticipate the future for what it can become.

(Tracy McNair)

Bring Her Back

We go about our daily lives getting caught up in them and settling for the status quo. Maybe its fear of the unknown that hinders our creative spirit, perhaps it is lack of motivation or just plain laziness. We seem to have so much on our plates that we forget who and what we intended to be. We become comfortable, complacent with what and who we are, disregarding our daring dreams, abandoning our gregarious goals, putting living in the moment on mute. We lose our childish charm. Sad, isn't it? We simply stop growing. It can happen to any woman, at any age, educational level, familial background, financial or marital status. It just happens.

Laughter does not tickle our tummies nor do smiles curl our lips near often enough. We don't listen or move our bodies to our favorite music anymore. Have we begun to take ourselves too seriously? Have we left the little girl way too far behind? Bring her back!

This is the internal part of the Divalution. It will be easier to have strength in numbers if you are secure within yourself.

This is the time when a woman must make an "all holds barred" self assessment, stand in front of a mirror and look herself in the eye and ask "Am I all I ever wanted to be"? It will be painful. It may be sad. (My wish for you is that it will be joyous . . . or will be someday soon.)

Weight is not the issue, health and self worth are. Please, learn to love who you are right now!

Bring yourself back to life. Consider yourself just waiting to bust free of your cocoon. Start now. Make a list of everything you imagined yourself to be at this stage of your life. Not where you wanted or expected to be, but who you wanted to be, your idyllic image. Search deeply. Remember. We are here for a reason. What's yours? Be honest. Do not cast blame, only assess.

Now prioritize. Start with easy steps that will bring quick obvious results. Dance, laugh till you cry. Un-snob and purge yourself of grudge holding, blame and pettiness. No more gossiping, back stabbing or making disparaging remarks. Hold your stomach in, shoulders back and head high. Take some time to do your toes and shave your legs. Color your hair a color you've been shy to try. Let go of the past. What's happened happened. Let it go. Release the butterfly.

There is a current you and a new you that will emerge. The old you will try to interfere and interrupt your metamorphosis, do not let her. Purge yourself of grudges. Rid yourself of guilt. Point the finger at only you take full responsibility of who you choose to be. Take a deep breath, let it out and forgive.

That is what it's all about FORGIVENESS. It does matter who, when or where. You just have to let it go.

Allow your inner Diva to evolve! Set her free.

My Thoughts

Deborah St.Hilaire

Paint a picture of the new and improved you:

What I need to forgive:

How the new me looks:

My style defined:

How I want others to see me:

Phase One: Take immediate actions

Deborah St.Hilaire

Immediate Results:

Phase Two: Three month action plan

Short Term Results:

Phase Three: Six month action plan

Mid Range Results:

Phase Four: One year action plan

Long Term Results:

Final Results:

The Diva I Am Today:

Deborah St.Hilaire

Make a dream board. Cut pictures from magazines. Draw on pictures of you. It's yours, Make it that way.

Forgive, forget and free your inner beauty. Look yourself in the eye and say "I love you".

Don't be afraid of this journey. Start sooner than later, you'll have more time. Take a friend with you. Remember we are here to be supportive of each other!

You will notice subtle differences at first. A smile will soften you lips, a giggle will creep up for no apparent reason, a new friend from an old acquaintance, politeness from strangers. Your altered, divalutioned self will grow more and more evident from the tips of your well manicured fingers to the tips of your polished toes to your perfect hair do. Don't ask me why.

You will just fit!

My Divalutionized Dream

Diva Devastation

In The late seventies I hung around with a group of five unmanned women. We were all in our late to mid twenties, made decent money with unique looks and above average intelligence. We were neighbors in Auburn, California, a small town in the Sierra foothills. We hiked together, worked together and partied together.

Once a month we would dawn our girl clothes and head to a fancy restaurant. We would sip martinis and eat escargot, drink hearty red wines and dine on fillet mignon. A flaming desert and a snifter of fine cognac would wind down the evening.

One of our favorite places was Epomonanda's, near Sacramento. It attracted the "yuppie" crowd, couples as well as suited young business men. The "suits" usually sat at the bar smiling and laughing, gawking at the women that entered, as they drank their imported beers. We looked especially hot, that spring evening, glowing with youthful vibrancy from spending the day swimming and hiking at the American River.

I can still close my eyes and picture us. We all stood out for various reasons: Diana with her six foot frame and curly flaming red hair,

Julie with her mass of dark curls framing an angelic face, Karen with her blond hair and flowing graceful manner, Carmen's Jersey accent and kinky black hair, Tara with her exotic beauty, dark eyes and tons of gold jewelry and me with a deeply tanned athletic body. My new dress was a silk skimpy little black Hawaiian print number with skinny straps and a slit up the front. We all wore strappy sandals, most of us just panties some panty hose. As a group, people noticed us. None of us were beautiful, but we were stunning.

When we walked into that restaurant, heads turned. We were seated, had a cocktail and decided to go to the ladies room before the appetizer came. As we returned to our table, people stopped eating or gazing at each other to stare at us as we passed. Over my shoulder, I said to Diana, "wow, we must really look good". We were reseated when our adorable puppy dog eyed waiter leaned into our table and whispered in Julie's ear "your dress is stuck up in your panty hose". She reached under her elevated bum and sure enough, it had been exposed for all to see. Tears came to her eyes as she turned a shade of pink I had never seen before or since. She was devastated! She sat perfectly still staring down at her napkin, for about fifteen seconds. Then, with a big grin, announced "let's eat".

After a yummy meal we drank snifters of brandy finished our chocolate mousse, then calmly hoisted our dresses into our panties or nylons. We arose simultaneously, held our heads high and walked out single file.

Several months passed before we made a daring return. As we were seated, that adorable waiter brought us an expensive bottle of California Cabernet "on him". Much to our delight, he tasted, poured and raised his glass toasting "to six classy women."

This was one of the most Divaistic events of my life. This is what we do for each other. I do not mean to man bash, but no male would expose his soul let alone his rear in order to re elevate a devastated Diva. That's what it is all about. We are there for one another, no matter the circumstances or the consequences.

Later that summer, Julie was killed in a small plane accident piloted by her fiancée' on their way to a fine dining experience in northern California. She is now deservingly immortalized as the beautifully kind hearted Diva she truly was.

The moral of this story is a simple one: Be there through thick and thin. It may be the last time.

Deborah St.Hilaire

To Be A Diva

To be a Diva is to be at one with yourself. Not at peace, for we are forever striving to improve, both internally and externally. You must become simultaneously aware of your roots and your metamorphosing wings. You must recognize your strengths as well as your weaknesses, where they came from and why. You must learn from your mistakes and not repeat them. You must realize that you have the power to create your own destiny and have the guts to do so.

Being a Diva requires a vast amount of responsibility. We have been around since the dawn of woman-time. We have been referred to as Shivas, Shaw-women, earth mothers, oracles, priestesses, witches, bitches and head strong ball busters. We are the women who fought for equality; now that we have it we must unite and learn how to manage it. At times it will be overwhelming. The expectations that others place on us will be nearly as great as our own.

The purpose of the Divalution is to unite us. Together we have and will continue to attain the unattainable. As one, in Divahood, we can reach the highest of the fruit and feast upon it!

My Thoughts

Deborah St.Hilaire

The Divalutionary Dream

There is a dream in every woman's heart to do something great, to achieve the impossible. To reach a personal height never reached before. We strive to do and be our best, no matter how menial the task or how irrelevant the project may appear to others. We are dreamers of the unattainable, doers of the unimaginable and givers to the ungiftable.

We want the best for everyone, especially our children and those we love. We long for peace and tranquility. We desire to shelter the homeless, feed the hungry, nurture the orphaned, right the wronged and comfort, if not cure, the sick. We hold hands and dance with the young as well as the old. We smile at the grumpy and joke with people who hate their jobs. We laugh at our own blunders but never those of others, unless they laugh first.

We are strong yet gentle, stern yet kind, insistent yet polite.

We are not judgmental nor do we gossip. We dress for the occasion, always elegantly understated.

We are lovers of the arts yet enjoy an occasional drag race. We adore flip flops yet look fabulous in heels. Our clothes are stylish yet not too trendy. Our hair can be any color we desire.

However, above all else, we are not back stabbers. We do not say anything behind another person's back we would not say to their face. We do not use another as a stepping stone, without the other's knowledge. (There are those who are content in their current position and are willing to be trod upon) We are kind and welcoming to the "newbie", hoping that they, too, are aware of the Divalutionary Laws.

Our dream can come true. Teach, mentor and share through example. Together, we change the world.

Deborah St.Hilaire

Divalutionary
Universal Truths

Divalutionary Universal Truths

1. There is never any justification for domestic violence.

2. Dancing is good for the body, mind and soul.

3. A parent should love their child unconditionally and vice versa.

4. Gravity and aging are not our friends and should be combated accordingly.

5. There is nothing a glass of fine red wine won't cure.

6. True love should be a verb not a noun.

7. You are never too old to look your best, fall in love, dream, learn something new or try a new recipe.

8. Amicable divorce is an oxymoron.

9. A female can do anything a male can do but shouldn't.

10. Never go grocery or jeans shopping on an empty stomach. You'll end up with stuff you don't want.

11. A best friend is a precious commodity and should be treated with great care.

12. There is no such thing as a gaudy diamond.

13. With age comes wisdom and gray hair. Let it grow out when you feel that you have earned it.

14. Make up is not supposed to look "made up" but to enhance and conceal.

15. Dressing and acting your age should not be chronologically based.

16. There's nothing sexier than a soft flannel night gown on a cold winter's night.

17. Candle light is flattering.

18. A marvelous cook is a living legacy.

19. There is no such thing as a bad day.

20. The size (areas of coverage) of your bathing suit should be chronologically based.

21. You do not have to eat everything on your plate.

22. Fish net stockings are not attractive.

23. A good bra is a wardrobe essential. Wear it!

Deborah St.Hilaire

24. There are times when cleavage is not appropriate. Learn them!

25. Even if you have a horrible voice, it's okay to sing loudly, when you're alone.

26. Live without regrets.

1. Domestic Violence

If you ever know or hear of a woman in an abusive relationship, help her!!!

The abuse could be verbal, mental and/or physical.

It does not matter who she is or how you feel about her. What does matter is that she needs someone, immediately. It may appear that she does not want assistance from you or anybody else. She wears a mask. Permeate it.

Who would help you? Who knows you well enough? Who would you trust?

Put yourself in her place.

She has little emotional strength . . . Her self esteem and worth is plummeting down a bottomless pit. She may be afraid for her children. She lives in constant fear for herself. Chances are she suffers from anxiety, depression, sleep deprivation and God knows what else. Is she staying because of finances? He has probably convinced her that she and the children cannot make it without him. She may actually think she still loves him and he will stop. He will not. She may not have anyone to turn to. Be that someone. Do something. Throw her a rope. Lift her.

Remember, there is no excuse! Divas help others.

2. The Dance

Feeling blue, burdened, burned out or besieged? Dance.

When moving to your favorite music, your troubles just disappear. It's a good way to start the day, energize your afternoon or purge yourself of a stressful job at day's end. You cannot be sad, mad or upset while dancing. Try it.

It's one of the reasons I love weddings so much. Dads dance with daughters, mothers with sons, and grandparents with grandchildren. My favorite is grandpas with grandmas; they can anticipate the next move with such grace and charm. Then everyone forms a line and dances together. Each person is smiling and laughing, which father illustrates my point. Weddings are glorious events.

You can dance any time any where! Turn up the music and let it rock your soul and soles. Melt your melancholy; lose your listlessness, live!!!

Dancing with friends is really fun!

Thanks to Ellen DeGeneres, aerobics and portable music, women are dancing more.

It soothes your body, mind and soul. Do it often, with feeling!

Deborah St.Hilaire

3. Unconditional Love

We may not always agree with the choices or opinions of those we love the most, but we always love them. We have learned that we cannot force our will upon another person. We are not afraid to give our honest opinion or advice, when asked, but do not "unlove" if it is not followed.

The following quote, from Thomas Merton, is especially applicable for the love of our children and life partner.

"The beginning of love is to let those we love be perfectly themselves, and not to twist them to fit our own image. Otherwise we love only the reflection of ourselves we find in them."

No matter what, love unconditionally! It may be painful at times. Tears beat the alternative, for there will also be tears of utter joy and pure pride.

A Diva can be selfish but when it comes to loving her family she is selfless. I have seen it so many times. Look around you, it is there.

Within this love lies the hope for womankind.

4. Gravity and Aging

We get droopy! We gaze in the mirror one day to see a face we hardly recognize. We catch a glimpse of the once firm young body and grimace. It happens to the best of us. What should we do about it? Fight it.

I managed a women's health club in Auburn, California. It was a time when a woman "working out" was just coming into vogue. It was there that I met Tamara Sudsloff, a tiny, wrinkled octogenarian with the sparkling eyes of a child. How I loved her. She spoke with a Russian accent very similar to my grandfather's. I was the only one that could carry on a conversation with. We became very good friends over the years. She often invited me for tea or lunch. She lived in the guest house on her daughter's property. It was the perfect size and decorated with an old world charm that both warmed and enchanted me. I found comfort in the burgundy and muted greens with white lace curtains and lush green plants. I loved it there.

She walked through the mirrored aerobics room every day on her way out of my club, but on this particular day, I saw her jump. She was visibly shaken as she approached me. I asked her what was wrong. To this day I will never forget her tearful response "I can't believe that old woman is me, I still feel like little girl". She was a Diva.

Judy Collins said it best, "I look in the mirror through the eyes of the child that was me."

Keep that child alive. Stay fluid, stretch, dance, breathe deeply, walk, lift weights, smile, laugh hard and often, love, cry, befriend younger women. If you want cosmetic surgery, go for it!

A Divalutionary woman will grow old gracefully, fighting it every step of the way!

5. Fine Wine

When all else fails, have a glass of red wine!

Red wine is actually good for you, in moderation of course. It is loaded with antioxidants plus it contains resveratrol. It is good for your skin and heart not to mention your mental health.

Resveratrol might be a key ingredient in red wine that can help prevent damage to blood vessels reduces "bad" cholesterol and raises "good". The reason it is only found in red wines is because it found mainly in the skins. There are flavonoids that act as antioxidants to help prevent blood clots and plaque formation in your arteries.

That should be reason enough to make red wine your drink of choice. It is a thoughtful gift as well. It rounds out a splendid meal and encourages conversation.

So, you Divas, raise your glass and toast to . . . whatever . . .

6. True Love

I believe that every person has more than one true love.

I believe that it is more important to love truly. It's like that old song says ". . . love the one you're with".

You may be lucky enough to stay in love with the same partner for many years, even a lifetime, but if not, no regrets, just make certain to truly love the person you choose to be with at this moment.

Give it your all. Share your dreams. Talk. Laugh. Drink red wine.

If you are fortunate enough to evolve together, good for you!

"Truly loving another means letting go of all expectations. It means full acceptance, even celebration of another's personhood."

Karen Casey

Celebrate that relationship. Nurture your togetherness. Grow together.

7. You're never too old . . .

The Divalutionary woman will never stop doing the things she is passionate about. She is open to new experiences and relationships. She does not fear change and longs to expand her horizons. She has fun.

Not matter her age, she takes pleasure in preparing and sharing an excellent meal with a fine wine pairing, of course.

She will always adore wearing a gown and find comfort in sweats.

Learning, discovering and trying new things will forever be a priority.

She knows that when she stops growing, she will be old; she fights to stay young . . . at heart.

This woman stands out in a crowd. She is self aware, makes the most of her shell, appears to be much younger than she is, and is usually smiling or laughing.

This woman is a Diva.

You have seen her, know her, be her.

P.S. This woman was my mother.

Deborah St.Hilaire

8. Divorce

You weren't friends when you were married but as a divorced parent you are forced to eventually become "friendly" with your X.

However, know that during the divorce process friendship is impossible. The two of you have to agree, something you are not accustomed to. Your children have got to be more important than anything else. Their happiness and security must be paramount. For the sake of your children, this is a time when both parents must become selfless.

This is not a time for game playing or manipulation. This is a time for healing. Get it over quickly so the healing can commence.

There is no such thing as an amicable divorce. Once the finger pointing, tears and arguing are behind you, there is a whole new life ahead. You will eventually settle into an uncomfortable relationship, but it will take some time. There is such a thing as a working relationship. Let's call it amicable parenting.

Keep looking ahead and hey, have a glass of red wine.

If there are no children, heal you and skip ahead to the glass of wine.

9. A Female can do anything

As a Divalutionary woman, you are well aware of your strengths and the fact that you can accomplish anything you set your mind to. There are times however, when you need to sit back and let someone else do little somethings for you.

We are not limited by gender specific tasks, for there is no such thing. We must remember that men want to take care of us, as will our children in time. They will even want to pamper us upon occasion. Indulge them.

I, personally, have found this to be very difficult at times. I was single for many years and became accustomed to doing things for myself, my way. It took a lot of effort to allow a man to do things for me and even more effort not to redo things my way. I guess what finally allowed me to allow was seeing the gratification on my husband's face, on my son's face. They felt so proud that they had done something for me that I gave in and let them. It is easier now. I see that they do it because they love me and want to take care of me, not because they expect something in return.

Let go. Let them

10. Never go shopping on an empty stomach

When we are hungry, we feel skinny. Our stomachs feel flatter. Those "just a tad too tight" jeans seem as though they'll fit by tomorrow . . . if we don't eat. But then we see food.

The nasty snacks we know we shouldn't have get justified into our basket by not hads for ages. You know the ones. They are usually fried or involve cheese or chocolate.

Don't fall for the ploys of that devil on your shoulder in a leotard. He is leading you down the path of never fits and shouldn't eats.

Walk away! Run to the fruits and vegetables or the red wine isle.

11. A best friend . . .

Every woman should have a best friend, be them male or female.

There should be a person in whom you can confide without fear of judgment or ridicule. Someone that you can depend on for anything at any time. A person who knows your strengths and weaknesses and loves you because you are you.

This person should be treated as though they were a precious gem. You, in return, will be treated the same.

I look back at my best friends with such fondness and admiration for putting up with me through thick and thin. It amazes me how absolutely fortunate I have been when it comes to the subject of friends.

I still have two of my high school best friends, Carol and Kath. We do not see each other that often but when we do it is as no time has passed. They even still look the same.

There have been many best friends throughout my life, Tara, Prisca, Christine, Mary Kay, Don, and Susan. How I love them! They are

Deborah St.Hilaire

as important to me as my family is. My family has to love me, they choose to. That makes them all the more precious.

If you do not have a best friend, cultivate old and new relationships until you grow one.

It is well worth the time and energy spent.

P.S. I have to include my cousin, Jeanne, too. We share more hilarious memories than anyone else.

As I was working on this book, I received a very welcome surprise from an old best friend. It had been nearly ten years since we had last spoken. I welcome her back into my life with gratitude. I missed her. Thanks for the call, Prisca. You warmed my heart.

I am now in touch with nearly all of them, except Karin and Kay. How grateful I am!!! How lucky!!!

12. There is no such thing as a gaudy diamond...

Or any gem, for that matter.

It's the attitude of the wearer that makes it gaudy.

Flaunting is highly discouraged, under any circumstance. You know other women can see it, perhaps even inquire about it. Tell the truth and move on to the next subject. No big deal. Right? You just happen to have a man who can afford you.

However, there is one exception: the newly engaged. Then and only then should the finger be exhibited without inquiry. This is the one time in your life when you can display your jewelry, without hesitation, well, to just about anyone you should meet. Have some fun!

The rest of the time, wear it proud yet humble. You deserve it.

13. With age comes wisdom and gray hair.

When is the right time to let it go gray? I am still asking myself this question.

I observe women that look just fine with colored hair well into their 70s and 80s. There are, as well, women that are prematurely grey who look fantastic.

I so admire Jamie Lee Curtis. She is strong and secure in her own skin and gray hair. Perfect example of a Diva.

To color or not to color is a very personal decision. It is how you picture yourself. It is the image you want to project. It is your essence.

This has been a great concern of mine for some time now. I have recently come to the conclusion that I will continue to color my hair, as close to my natural color without being too dark, until I feel as though gray hair would go better with my face. When that day comes, I will get it cut short (I despise that gray root look) and let it go. It will be very brave for me. It frightens me to think about it.

I figure I will, hopefully, be wise by then so why not show it off!!

14. Make up should be worn but not seen . . .

There is a place for the "made up" look, Las Vegas for example. A night on the town, all dressed up and decked out, maybe on your wedding day or if you are just having some fun or in need of a change.

I'm talking about your everyday look, office, base ball practice, running errands. You know what I mean. It looks fake. It looks as though you are hiding behind a false façade.

Let's face it, if you are trying to cover a blemish, disguise a receding chin or hide the fact that you have a big nose . . . hello, we can see it . . . it's not working! May I suggest that you play up your best feature, your eyes or cheek bones perhaps?

Remember, be yourself. Be comfortable in your own skin. Love what and who you are. God made you this way.

If you are that unhappy about the appearance of one particular facet of your face, save up for plastic surgery. Have a little work done. Just don't get carried away. Do not lose yourself in search of the perfect shell.

Work on the inside and the outside will become more beautiful.

People are attracted to your inner Diva. Your friends love your smile, your wit, your ideas, they love you. I'll bet they couldn't tell you what color top you had on the last time you were together but I'll bet they remember something that you laughed about or some insightful piece of wisdom you laid on them. That is what is important.

Never confuse looking your best with being your best. This is key for young women. Do not hide behind makeup. Develop your Divatude, your spirit. Be real. Be you.

Let makeup show YOU off, not you show off the makeup.

15. Dressing and acting your age should not be chronologically based.

Now I'm not saying that all grandmas have to follow every trend or every young woman must wear the tiniest bikini possible. I am saying find a comfortable style and make it your own.

Take a navy blue blazer for example. A timeless piece, a wardrobe essential. It can be worn at any age. A young woman might wear it with a little short skirt, an older woman with a white shirt and jeans or a skirt for the office. It's a good look. Heck, I wore one every day for four years in high school. LOL

My point is your taste does not have become old with you. Once you turn forty you don't have to start shopping in the old lady section . . . unless you have always shopped there. If that's the case, all righty then. You have found your style niche.

Wear what makes you feel and look your best. Be comfortably at ease in your wrappings. Of course your taste will mature but your sense of style will remain constant.

Deborah St.Hilaire

Never try to look twenty years younger. That's just tacky and unDivalutionary. We can all tell how old you are. That look makes us cringe.

Keep it simple, understated and elegant. Keep it true to yourself. Keep it real.

The exception being when you're at home. You can wear whatever, whenever!!

16. A sexy soft flannel night gown

Ah, a cold winter's night, a roaring fire, a glass of red wine, on a flacotti, in your favorite flannel night gown with the one you love. Really, does it get any better than that? I don't think so.

I saw this white one once. It was so soft, as though it had been washed a hundred times. It had a small round color and tiny pink buttons with pin tucking and a little gather in the back. It was gorgeous. I was Christmas shopping and I make it a rule not to buy for me when doing so. I am still kicking myself in the ass for not buying that night gown. I gifted it to my lovely niece, Kate.

I wonder if she still has it.

The moral of that story is: If you find the perfect flannel night gown get two, one as a gift and one for yourself.

Deborah St.Hilaire

17. Candlelight is flattering

I don't know why we don't use it more often. It softens our mood as well as our features.

Posh restaurants use candle light. That should tell us something. Anyone appears smoother. Food even looks better. It is romantic. It implores you to hold hands and gaze lovingly into each other's eyes.

OK, maybe I am getting a little carried away here but I have never heard anyone complain about having too much romance in their lives. I'm just saying, hey, what would it hurt to have a little candle lit dinner every now and then?

If you are a safety freak, the electric candles are amazing these days. Unscented at the dinner table, please.

A Divalutionary woman changes it up, keeps it interesting and dimly lit.

18. A marvelous cook is a living legacy

Cook for your children when they are young and they will visit you often as they grow up.

Teach your children to cook. You will be with them their entire lives, as will their children. Around the table will be heard "this is mom's, or grandma's, recipe."

I grew up in a catering family. I learned to cook from grandma, my mother, and her sisters. Each one had their specialty. When I was tall enough to reach the counter tops, I was educated in chopping, dicing and mincing. I was spice schooled and flavor informed. Everything I make is delicious. Thanks mom. She would have loved my husband, Steve. He relishes every bite.

I knew I had succeeded when each of my sons' live-in girlfriends thanked me for teaching them how to cook. I have passed it down, boys, keep it going. Hint hint.

I am not with my family as often as I would like but when we are, we're cooking! We have fun in the kitchen. It's what we do. I just love it!

Our food is Divalicious!

P.S. Cook for your step-children and they will grow to love you.

Deborah St.Hilaire

19. There is no such thing as a bad day . . .

. . . the day is what you make it, choose to make it a good one.

Think about the "Law of Attraction", what you dwell on will come to be, be it positive or negative. Make it positive.

That's easy to say, but I know you can do it. There are so many different ways. Here are but a few:

- Have a happy memory, complete with emotional charge, on standby at all times. Don't be afraid to use it.

- Close your eyes take a few deep breaths and let **it** go.

- I'll tell you one that works well for me on several different levels. When something goes wrong, I become extremely aware of what is going to happen after that. One morning, my blow dryer broke before I was finished using it. Need I say more? This forced me into a different do than I was planning, thus making me late for an appointment. I had to slow myself down and pay attention to what I was doing so that something else would not go wrong because of my haste. I was about fifteen minutes late. On my way, police cars, a fire truck and an ambulance passed me. Up ahead there was a car that had sped through a stop sign hitting another in the driver's door. That could have been me.

- Go for a walk.

- Have a nice long bubble bath and cry, if you need to.

- Dance to your favorite song.

- Have a glass of red wine at the end of the day. Another one of my favorites.

Anyway, when your day starts off badly either go back to bed or turn it around.

20. Now let's talk about the size of our bathing suits . . .

Unlike most everything else, the size of a bathing suit should be chronologically based. The older the woman the more affected by gravity the more coverage a bathing suit (as well as other clothing) should provide.

I mean, really, ladies, as you age you should become a tad more modest, when in public. Kind of like the cleavage thing.

Run around naked at home!

New rule of thumb: The older you get, the more you should cover but you can always be nakey at home. 2012

21. You do not have to eat everything . . .

On your plate, take it home in a doggie bag. LOL

We were all taught to clean our plates. Some of you have overcome this. I'm still working on it. It is difficult not to over eat at dinner. It is my one big meal and it is scrumptious! Maybe a smaller plate would help.

Do try to eat nutritious foods. Avoid empty calories. Eat when you are hungry and stop when you are full.

Sounds like a new rule of thumb to me!

Deborah St.Hilaire

22. Fish net stockings are not attractive . . .

I don't care how young or how thin you are, stuff creeps out between those diamonds and it is not attractive. It's gross.

This has been a self imposed rule for over forty years now. I believe that puts it in the ranks of a Divalutionary truth. See 22 ½.

Now I am going to tell you why. I was traumatized by fishnet stocking as a young artist taking a studio class from a thirty something, slightly hippie-ish instructor. Oh, it was terrible. She was just the fat side of skinny and oh how she loved her fish nets. She had every color. She wore them daily. At least once a week she would set up a still life. She always faced her ass in our direction. It was like she wanted us to look. There it was, skin bulging its way through the tiny rope diamonds. Sometimes I thought one would burst. Ugh, I can still feel the common disgust. Even the guys would cover their eyes. She ruined them for me. Now I am spoiling them for you.

A Diva only wears fish nets with a long skirt as part of a Halloween costume. Consider this a new rule of thumb.

22 ½. Once a rule of thumb holds true for forty years, it becomes a universal, and in some cases, a Divalutionary truth.

23. A good bra should be worn

. . . whenever you are expecting company or out of your house.

There was a time when that was not true. In the late sixties and early seventies I doubt that anyone under the age of 25 wore one religiously. Hell, they were burning them. They must have been much less expensive in those days. They were pointy, binding and did not have any give. White cotton, two or three hooks, and they had to be ironed. A bra was often accompanied by a girdle and nylons. No wonder we revolted.

We united for a cause, just as we did to win the vote. Both were to overcome woman's suffrage. See, we can do it.

I digress.

The bra has changed. It now forms to fit bodies with comfort and ease. While we are on the subject, the racer back and strapless should be worn much more frequently than they are. I'm just saying.

So the next time you are leaving the house, take a final glimpse in the mirror. Look at the boobs, the bra and what's showing.

Deborah St.Hilaire

24. There are times when cleavage is not appropriate . . .

Know them. We really should make a list, keep track for forty years, and make the ones that have held true Divalutionary truths.

I will begin the list. We can add to it on Facebook. That would be fun. Remember to keep track of the year it was proclaimed.

1.   At your child's graduation or birthday party. 2012

2.   Any Little League event. 2012

3.   At funerals. 2012

4.   Most professional settings. The exceptions should also be noted.

     Exception #   1. If you are a hooker.

                    2. If you are a dancer.

                    3. If you are involved in show business.

Feel free to add to this list also.

Let's consider why your boob crack needs to concealed appropriately. Any time that it could potentially be embarrassing or uncomfortable for any party involved, keep it hidden.

Some men are unmindful enough to look at another woman's cleavage. Do not put a woman in that situation. This could hurt you in a professional setting, especially if the woman is the decision maker. Pay attention.

A child will pick up on the attention you receive. Dress for the occasion. Dress modestly for school and sporting functions.

It just isn't nice or polite sometimes. Just be aware, that is all I ask.

Deborah St.Hilaire

25. Sing loudly . . .

. . . even if you have an unpleasant singing voice (just do it alone).

Ya know, it just feels good to belt out the lyrics to a favorite song, even if you do not know all of the words. It's primal.

I, unfortunately, have a horrible singing voice. My sons both requested that I not sing them lullabies at a very early age. Since then, I sing loudly to the radio as I clean and when I am driving **alone** in both cases.

Somehow my sons got incredible singing voices. Must skip a generation.

If you are gifted with a pleasant voice, by all means sing whenever you can. It is something I have admired my whole life, when somebody just starts singing to a song and it sounds good. My sister surprised me when she sang aloud with Joni Mitchell (a Diva) for the first time. My sons to a Beach Boy song on the way to grandma's house. My friends, Christine and Carmen, sound like an angles. My son, Michael, sounds his father, and I still love to listen to him. LOL My husband, Steve, can even hit the high notes. It is fun to listen.

Sing whenever, wherever you can.

Accompany it with dance and a glass of wine when possible.

26. Live your life without regrets

Some messages are more difficult to convey than others, this is one of them, for we all have regrets of some type.

We have our "if onlys, I should haves, I could haves and why didn't I's". We carry them around with us and pull them out when something in our life is not going well. We tend to dwell upon them during times of duress. Those are the times I am talking about. You have to let them go.

Remember how "The Law of Attraction" works?

So, here you are, down in the dumps, reminiscing about everything that has gone wrong in your life. Get what I am saying?

We all make mistakes. It is part of life. Learn from them, try not to repeat them and move on. Grow.

You are who you are and you are where you are because of each decision, each person, each situation you have ever encountered. Be joyful for them or alter your future, starting today. You cannot change the past. You can create your future.

Deborah St.Hilaire

Smile more, help more, give more and take better care of yourself.

It is never too late to become the Diva you were meant to be!

Your past is not your potential. In any hour you can choose to liberate the future. (Marilyn Ferguson)

My Dear Reader,

The purpose of this book was to realign your brain with your heart. We have become cold, somehow. We have forgotten how to be women.

As you grow, educate your mind and feed your soul. Become whole.

If only we would all learn to nurture and love ourselves, we could do the same for others. We would mentor without jealousy, love without reservation and live without restriction.

My wish for you is that you become your best self, find someone who compliments that self and that you raise your children unspoiled, aware and kind.

My friends, Let the Divalutionary War begin!!!

Thank you.

Love,
Deborah

I leave you with this Divalutionary Truth:

The future depends on what we do in the present.

(Mahatma Gandhi)

The Beginning

www.ingramcontent.com/pod-product-compliance
Lightning Source LLC
Chambersburg PA
CBHW030350290526
45785CB00004B/1678